Drawing MONSTERS Step-by-Step

Drawing WITCHES and WIZARDS

I0892316

Carter Hayn

WINDMILL BOOKS
New York

Published in 2013 by Windmill Books, LLC

CREDITS:
Book Design: Nathalie Beullens-Maoui
Art by Planman, Ltd.

Photo Credits: Cover, p. 18 Joy Brown/Shutterstock.com p. 4 Christophe Testi/Shutterstock.com (pencil); p. 5 Obak/Shutterstock.com (paper), Paul Matthew Photography/Shutterstock.com (eraser), 2happy/Shutterstock.com (marker), Iv Nikolny/Shutterstock.com (pencils); p. 6 Photos.com/Thinkstock; p. 8 Virgil Apger/Moviepix/Getty Images; pp. 10, 12 © Warner Brothers/Courtesy Everett Collection; p. 14 Pierre Verdy/AFP/Getty Images; p. 16 Lori Martin/Shutterstock.com; p. 20 Jupiterimages/liquidlibrary/Thinkstock.

Cataloging-in-Publication Data

Hayn, Carter.
Drawing Witches and Wizards / by Carter Hayn.
p. cm. — (Drawing monsters step-by-step)
Includes index.
ISBN 978-1-61533-693-7 (library binding) —ISBN 978-1-61533-706-4 (pbk.) —
ISBN 978-1-61533-707-1 (6-Pack)
1. Witches in art — Juvenile literature. 2. Wizards in art — Juvenile literature. 3. Drawing — Technique — Juvenile literature. I. Title.
NC825.W58 H39 2013
743.4—dc23

Manufactured in the United States of America

CPSIA Compliance Information: Batch #BW13WM: For further information contact Windmill Books, New York, New York at 1-866-478-0556.

Contents

Witchcraft Makers

People have believed in witchcraft, or the magic created by witches and wizards since the time of the pharaohs in Egypt. Witches and wizards are people who cast **spells** and make **potions**. Some are mean and others are good.

They may carry **wands** to make things appear, fly on brooms, or simply appear and disappear at will. Witches and wizards have lived in our imaginations for a long, long time. Although they often scare us, we are all fascinated by the magic that they do.

Read on to learn more about them and to try some fun drawings!

YOU WILL NEED THE FOLLOWING SUPPLIES:

PAPER

PENCIL

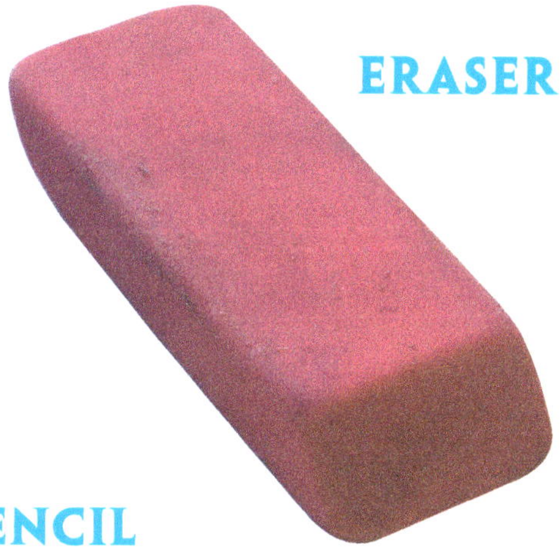

ERASER

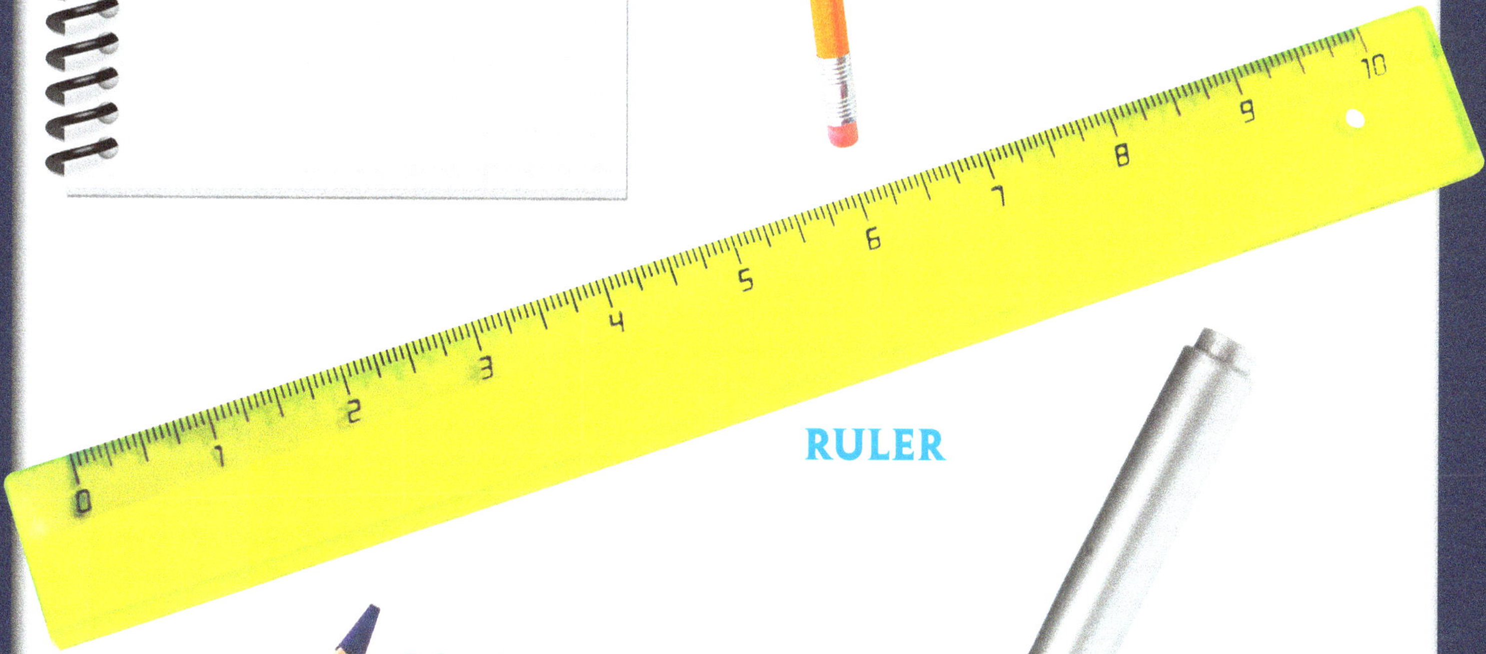

RULER

COLORED PENCILS

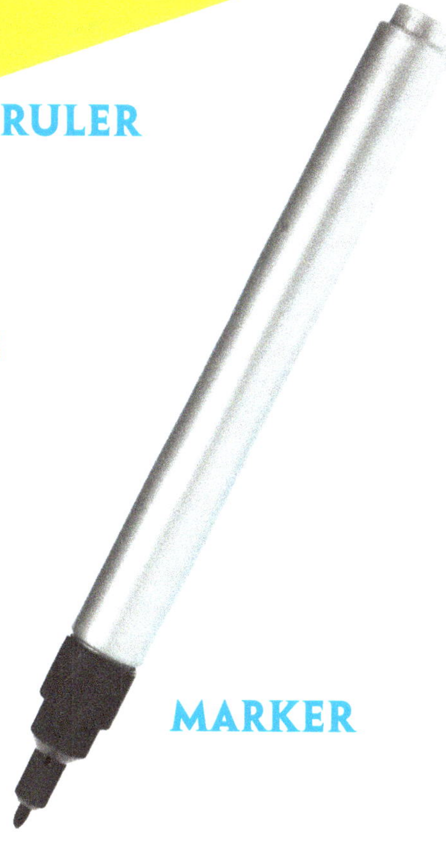

MARKER

One Ugly Witch

Mother Shipton lived in England from 1488 to 1561. She was known for telling the future. There are also stories about her terrifying appearance. Some people think she was a witch.

Stories say that Mother Shipton was born in a cave, in Yorkshire, England. It is now known as Mother Shipton's Cave. It is near a petrifying well that has been a tourist attraction since 1630.

As she grew older, her appearance became more frightening. She is said to have had a hooked nose, bumpy chin, and many warts.

In her later life, Mother Shipton lived in a cottage where people said they saw furniture and plates move by themselves. Food would disappear before their very eyes, too!

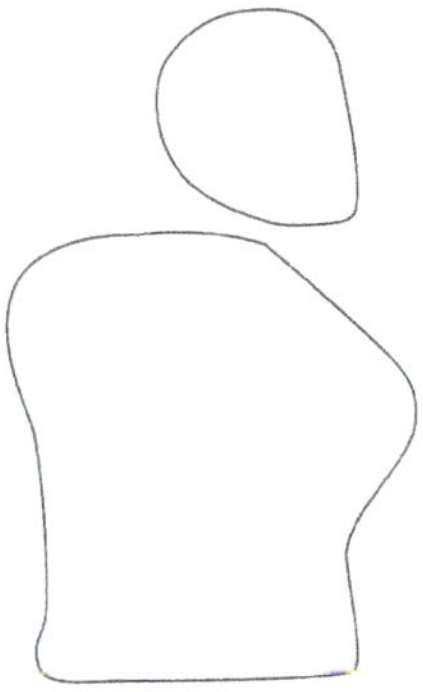

STEP 1

Draw the outlines of the head and the body.

STEP 2

Add small ovals as gudies for the arms.

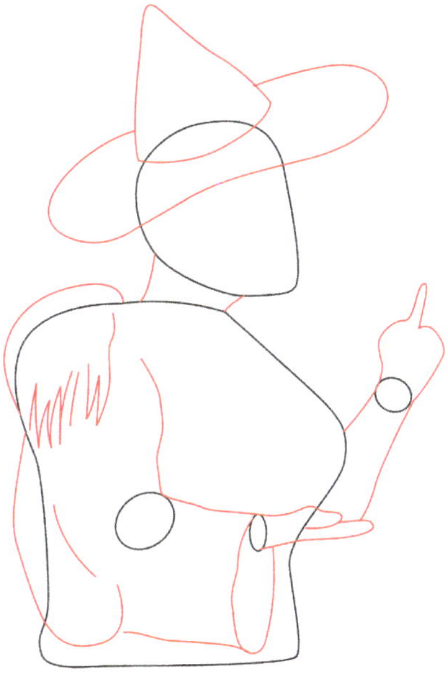

STEP 3

Use the ovals to draw the arms. Add the outlines of the hands and shoulder. Draw the outline of the hat. Add lines for the neck.

STEP 4

Draw the hairline, the nose, and the chin. Add details to the top of the dress. Draw the roll of paper.

STEP 5

Draw the eyes, the fingers and the hair on the chin. Add details to the clothes, face, paper, and hat.

STEP 6

Erase any extra lines and color your drawing.

A Wicked Witch

When we think of witches, the first things that come to mind are a pointed hat, a crooked nose, and long, **menacing** fingers. That's exactly how the witch in the movie *The Wizard of Oz* looked!

The Wicked Witch of the West, as her name implies, was a very wicked witch. She threw fireballs, cast spells, and sent winged monkeys to attack the movies heroine, Dorothy and her companions.

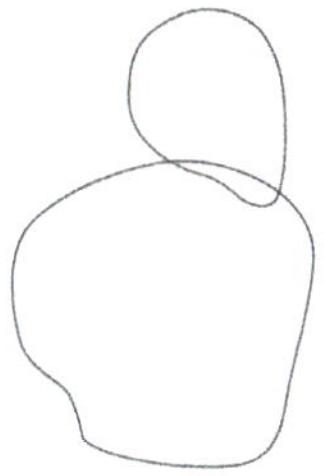

STEP 1
Draw shapes as shown to begin the head and body.

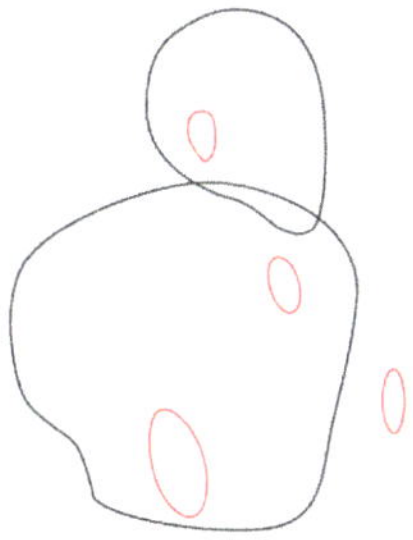

STEP 2
Draw small ovals around the body to act as guides for the arms, ear, and hands.

STEP 3
Use the ovals to draw the arms. Draw the hands and neck. Add the outlines for the hat and dress.

STEP 4
Draw the face, shoulders, fingers, and hair. Draw folds in the skirt and ribbons on the hat.

STEP 5
Draw the facial features. Add details to the hair, hands, and clothes. Erase guide ovals.

STEP 6
Erase all extra lines. Add details to the witch's face and dress. Add color.

The Boy Wizard

There are many famous wizards, but few as young as Harry Potter, from the series of novels by J. K. Rowling. In the first book, Harry Potter finds out that he is a wizard when he turns eleven years old. He becomes a gifted student at Hogwarts School of Witchcraft and Wizardy, a boarding school for witches and wizards.

Harry makes good friends at Hogwarts. He has many adventures, too. He eventually defeats an evil wizard called Lord Voldermort.

The Harry Potter books were turned into a series of movies. Daniel Radcliffe played Harry in all eight movies in the series. In this picture, he is wearing Harry's school uniform.

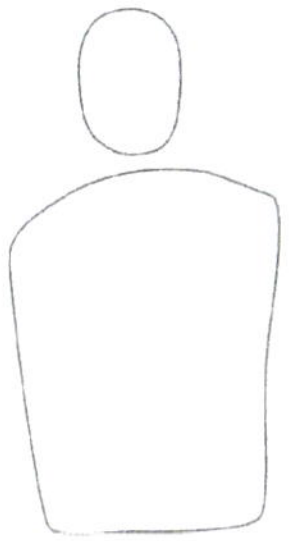

STEP 1

Draw a round shape for the head and a boxy shape for the body.

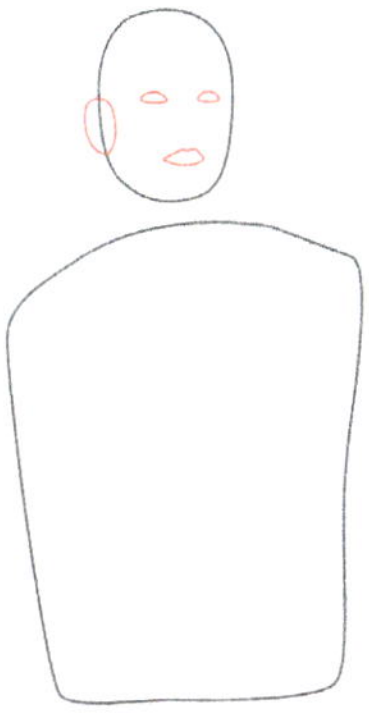

STEP 2

Draw ovals as guides the eyes, mouth, and ear.

STEP 3

Outline the hair as shown. Draw a line to serve as a guide for the body.

STEP 4

Draw the cape and scarf. Draw the sweater's collar and the tie as shown.

STEP 5

Draw eyes, eyebrows, nose, and mouth. Add the glasses. Add details to the clothes and hair.

STEP 6

Erase the guide shapes. Add more facial features. Draw more details to the clothing and color your drawing.

The Head Wizard

Michael Gambon played Professor Dumbledore in the later movies in the Harry Potter series.

Some wizards in stories use dark magic, but others believe that magic should be used for good. **Professor** Albus Percival Wulfric Brian Dumbledore is the perfect example of a good wizard. He is the headmaster of Hogwarts School of Witchcraft and Wizardy, where Harry Potter studies. Dumbledore is considered the most powerful wizard of his time. He knows many spells and can create objects with his magic wand. He is also good at making charms and potions. He even discovered the twelve magical uses of dragon's blood!

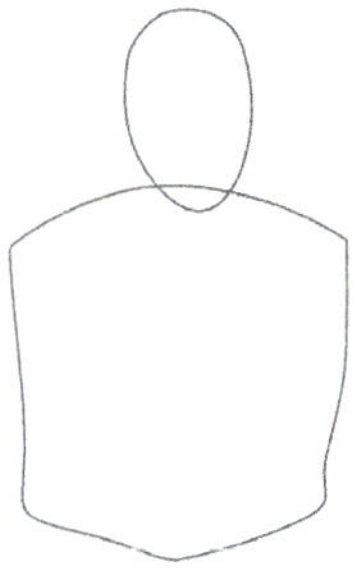

STEP 1

Draw the head and begin to draw the body.

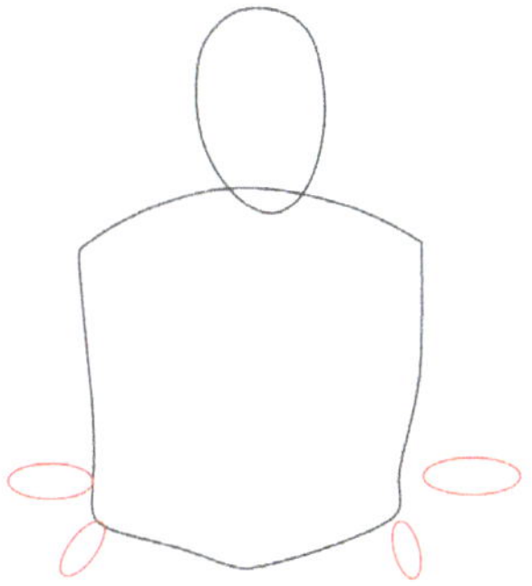

STEP 2

Draw ovals as shown. These will help you draw the arms.

STEP 3

Use the ovals to draw the hands and arms. Add the outlines of the hair and beard. Draw the bottom of the robe.

STEP 4

Draw the hat. Add details to the hands. Add details to the the robe as shown.

STEP 5

Add the eyes, eyebrows, nose, and mouth. Add details to the hair and hands. Draw the details of the robe and hat as shown.

STEP 6

Erase the guides. Add the final details to the face and the clothes. Color your drawing.

The Great Merlin

The wizard, Merlin is an important charater in the tales of King Arthur. Merlin was the king's guide and **adviser**.

Merlin was an extremely powerful wizard. He could see the future. He's also said to have been able to talk to animals and **communicate** with nature. Merlin was called a sorcerer, magician, and enchanter. Many plays and movies have been made about him. He is still a famous wizard to this day.

Legends about King Arthur and Merlin have been popular since the Middles Ages.

STEP 1
Draw a lopsided oval for the head. Add a shape for the outline of the upper body.

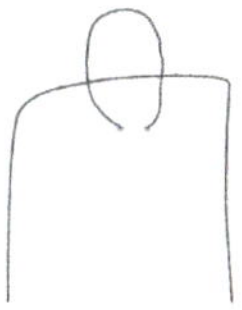

STEP 2
Draw the arms, hands, and outline of the lower body as shown.

STEP 3
Add the beard and hair. Draw the staff. Outline the fingers of each hand. Add the feet.

STEP 4
Draw the outline of the robe. Remember to include the long sleeves.

STEP 5
Draw the eyes, nose, and mouth. Add detail to the clothing.

STEP 6
Erase extra lines. Add more details to the face and clothes. Color your drawing.

A Classic Wizard

Drawings of Merlin have shaped our idea of how wizards look. They tend to be old men with long, white beards and long, white hair. Wizards often wear long robes, have a tall pointy hats, and use wands to make magic.

Popular belief states that a wizard's beard represents the power the wizard has. In European folklore, the more magic the wizard learns, the longer the beard is!

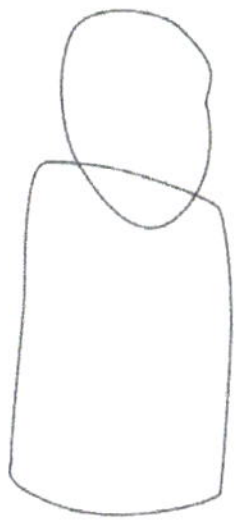

STEP 1

Begin your drawing with a lopsidedoval for the head an a boxy shape for the body.

STEP 2

Draw circle and oval guides for the arms. Draw the outlines of the ears.

STEP 3

Use the circles and ovals to draw the arms and hands. Add the beard, hair, and nose.

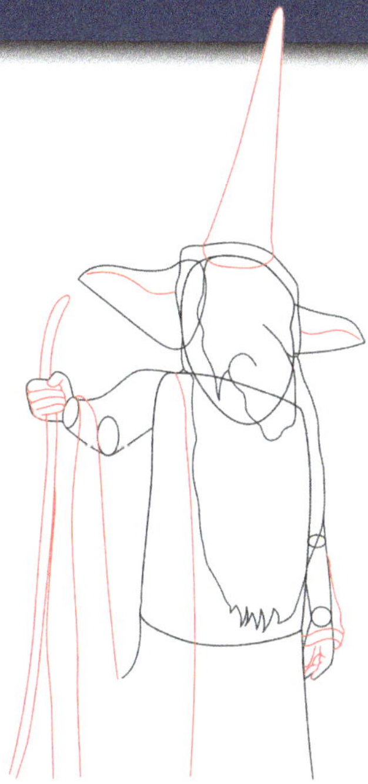

STEP 4

Draw the outline of the hat and the staff. Add the sleeves of the robe.

STEP 5

Draw the eyes. Add folds to the robe. Add more detail to the face, ears, and beard.

STEP 6

Erase extra lines. Add details to the facial features and clothing. Draw in greater detail to the beard. Color your drawing.

Classic Witches

Just like wizards, some witches were believed to use their magic for good, while others used dark magic. Good witches would brew potions to cure people, but bad witches used them for harm.

When thinking of witches, though, most people picture wicked witches. They are usually represented as ugly, old women, with crooked noses and warts. Some even have green skin! They tend to wear black dresses and pointy hats. and fly a broom.

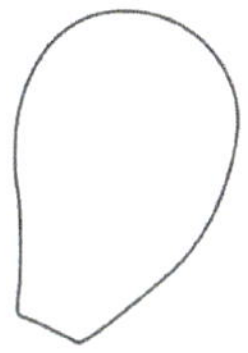

STEP 1
Draw the shape shown here for the head.

STEP 2
Add the nose. Draw the outline of the right arm.

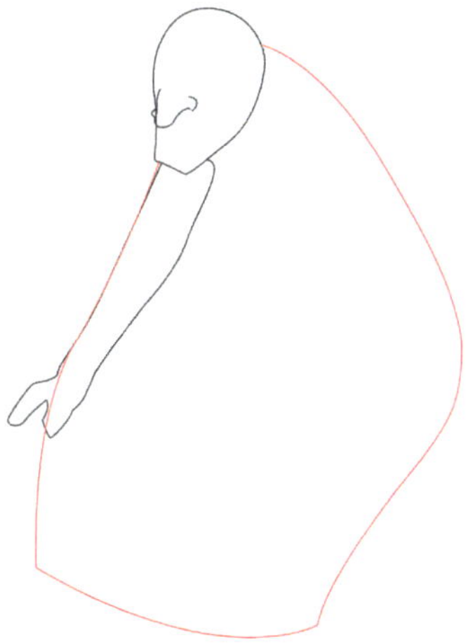

STEP 3
Draw the outline of the body as shown.

STEP 4
Draw the hat and broom. Add the outlines of the hair and clothes.

STEP 5
Draw the mouth. Add more detail to the hair, clothing, hat, and broom.

STEP 6
Erase extra lines. Add the final details to the face and clothes. Color your drawing.

Dungeons and Dragons

Wizards have always been important characters in role-playing games. One of those games is the very popular Dungeons and Dragons started in 1974 as an adventure game in which characters had different abilities. It has since become a complex game, which can also be played online.

One of the powers the wizards in Dungeons and Dragons have is the Irresistible Dance enchantment. It is a spell that makes the victim dance without being able to stop!

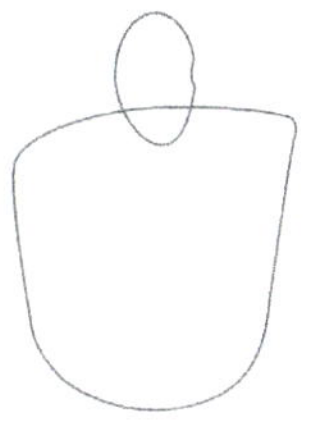

STEP 1

Draw the outlines of the head and body.

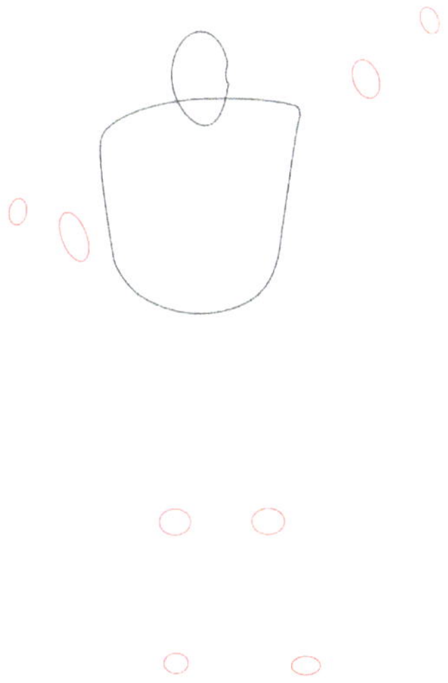

STEP 2

Add some ovals as guides for the arms and legs.

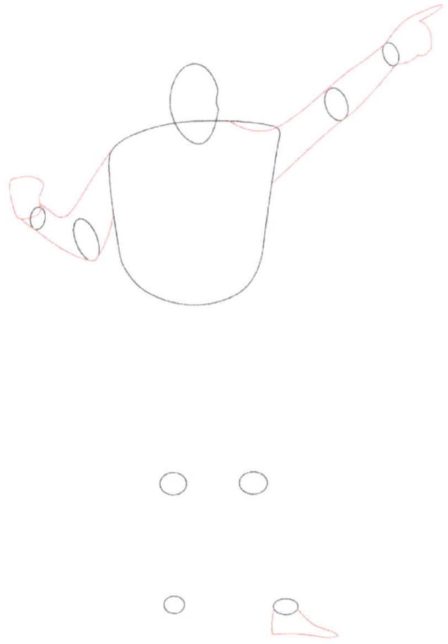

STEP 3

Use the ovals to draw the arms and hands. Draw the left foot.

STEP 4

Draw the outline of the cape over the head and behind the body. Draw the bottom of the robe. Add the sleeves and belt. Draw the beard.

STEP 5

Draw the staff and the lightning coming from the finger. Draw the wizard's face. Add more detail to the robe and cape.

STEP 6

Erase the guides and any other extra lines. Add finishing details and color your drawing.

Monster Fun Facts

- Almost every **culture** has a story about witches.
- While witches are usually female, some men have been named as witches, too.
- The word "wizard" comes from the Middle English word "wys," which means wise.
- The myth about flying on broomsticks most likely comes from an ancient festival where women would dance on a broom to make their crops grow taller.
- Most people believe that you cannot be born a witch. Witchcraft is studied and practiced.
- In the past, thousands of people were persecuted for witchcraft. Most were simply healers or midwives.

Glossary

ADVISER (ed-VY-zur) A person who helps another person make decisions.

COMMUNICATE (kuh-MYOO-nih-kayt) To share facts or feelings.

CULTURE (KUL-chur) The beliefs, practices, and arts of a group of people.

POTIONS (POH-shuns) Magical liquids.

MENACING (MEH-nuh-sing) Threatening harm.

PETRIFYING WELL (PEH-trih-fy-ing WEL) A well with water is said to make things turn to stone.

PROFESSOR (preh-FEH-ser) A teacher at a school for advanced students.

SPELLS (SPELS) Magical words that can make things happen.

WANDS (WONDS) Sticks or rods that are used to do magic.

Read More

Besel, Jennifer M. *Witches*. Mankato, MN: Capstone Press, 2006.

Curran, Robert. *The Wizards' Handbook: An Essential Guide to Wizards, Sorcerers, and Magicians and Their Magic*. Hauppauge, NY: Barron's Educational Series, Inc., 2011.

Ganeri, Anita. *Witches and Warlocks*. New York: PowerKids Press, 2011.

Index

Websites

For Web resources related to the subject of this book, go to:
www.windmillbooks.com/weblinks and select this book's title.